MW00654830

I know this to be true

NELSON MANDELA
FOUNDATION
Living the legacy

Ayesha Curry

I know this to be true

on family,
food &
community

Interview and photography
Geoff Blackwell

CHRONICLE BOOKS
SAN FRANCISCO

in association with

Blackwell&Ruth.

Dedicated to the legacy
and memory of
Nelson Mandela

'I've always been the girl who put things out into the air and put in the work to make them come to fruition. So I feel like you can hope and dream and wish, but until you do, nothing is going to happen. So whatever you're passionate about, whatever your hopes and dreams are, you have to go full-steam ahead.'

Introduction

When we approached Ayesha Curry to be part of the *I Know This to Be True* series, we were warmly invited to her office and studio in Oakland, California, USA. In a first act of generosity and trust, despite knowing there would be nobody there, we were given the building's entry code and told to go in as early as we like before the interview, take our time to set up, and make ourselves at home.

This initial kindness manifested in a dozen other ways. When she and her husband, Stephen, arrived, Ayesha immediately put us at ease with her relaxed, unaffected manner and natural warmth. All of us were seen, regardless of our role in the crew, and it seemed to us that this thoughtfulness is at the heart of who Ayesha Curry is.

The kindness continued when, after the interview, she worried whether we had somewhere to eat for dinner. Learning that we planned to dine at her San Francisco restaurant, International Smoke, she took the time to call the restaurant and ask them to bring us special desserts.

After our interviews, the Currys recorded a public service announcement for ESPN, before leaving to offer their support for an inspiring leader in the community who runs a boxing training facility for local underserved children. All part of the 'service before self' ethos that seems to come naturally to Ayesha Curry.

Food was a central part of her childhood while growing up in Toronto, Canada. An instrument that brought the family together, it gave them a chance to sit and connect. And it was exciting – simple, nutritious home cooking with vibrant flavour. 'My mom is Jamaican and Chinese, and my dad is Polish and African American, so I grew up in a kitchen full of all kinds of interesting flavour combinations', she explains.[1] With four siblings, she was expected to help around the house, and she chose cooking as her chore. It was the beginning of a long-lasting love affair with food.

After moving to the United States as a teenager, then-Ayesha Alexander met Stephen Curry at a church youth group. Banned from dating at the time, she took to sharing Canadian candy with Stephen to express her interest. When she graduated high school and moved to Los Angeles to pursue an acting career – appearing in several shows, including *Hannah Montana* and *Good Luck Charlie* – the budding relationship ended.

Several years later, however, they reconnected. Stephen was in town for basketball camp and reached out to Ayesha, who initially turned him down. Eventually they went on their first date, exploring the sites of Hollywood Boulevard and enjoying chai tea lattes. It was a success; in 2008 she made the move from Los Angeles to Charlotte, North Carolina, and two years later Stephen proposed.

It was only after leaving Los Angeles that Curry realized her true calling, and set her sights on a career in the food industry. It made sense; cooking was where her true passion lay. In a fast-paced world where eating-in and slow dining is a rarity, she wanted to share the experience she'd had as a child with others. 'It's becoming a lost art – people gathering at home, having fun, building memories. Growing up, that's all we did on the weekends. We weren't out at restaurants – we were at home in the comfort of our own space. I wanted to keep that alive.'[2]

She began her journey into the food world with the launch of *Little Lights of Mine*, a blog sharing homemade recipes, followed by a YouTube channel with cooking demonstrations. A cookbook, television show, cookware range and four restaurants later, it's fair to say Curry has found her footing. Despite the challenges of entering a male-dominated industry and the unavoidable negativity of cynics, she persevered and managed to create her own success. 'I've had people laugh directly in my face before. I had to break down so many barriers and walls and assumptions about the type of person that I was before I even walked into a room', she admits. 'Part of the dream and the hustle is ploughing through the no's to get to the yes's.'[3]

The belief that you work hard no matter what is key to Curry's philosophy. Equally important is a relentless positivity and a concern for the welfare of others. These elements combined inspired the launch of Eat. Learn. Play., the foundation she and Stephen co-founded in 2019. With two daughters and a son of their own, they wanted to ensure a better life for disadvantaged children. Eat. Learn. Play. provides support for youth by helping them access healthy food, quality exercise and education.

She leads without motivational speeches or grand gestures, but with an unfaltering commitment to service, kindness and authenticity. She uses her platform to create good, whether by helping children in need or bringing people joy and togetherness through cooking. Ultimately, in all aspects of her life, she highlights the importance of benevolence and care.

'As a woman of colour, it's important to me that media reflects real, relatable women.'

Prologue

I don't come from a traditional culinary background; I'm self-taught. I've found great mentors along the way, but I did not take the path of going to traditional culinary school. Do I wish I had? Sometimes, yes, some days, no. I think everything's turned out okay. But you work with what you have, and you do the best with what you've got, and you build on that.

I've been in entertainment doing commercial work since the age of three. My first official job – when I was three – I played the bubble elf in the movie *The Santa Claus* with Tim Allen. You can't see me in it, I'm nowhere to be found, but that was my first job. My first *real* job – I actually had three jobs at once – I worked at Abercrombie & Fitch, I worked at a frozen yoghurt shop, and then on weekends, I worked at a vegan food stand at a farmers' market. And I'm not vegan.

I've always had a passion for theatre, but I graduated high school a year early and moved out to Los Angeles to pursue an acting career. Everything was going great. I always had a job, I was always working, but it got to the point where I had dreams of being a Disney Channel star. Just after I moved out here [to the United States], I turned eighteen, and the stuff that was coming in was a little bit different and I wasn't prepared for it. I was a very sheltered child, and so everything was new to me. It got to the point where I just didn't want to have to sacrifice my morals; I was getting stuck in roles that I didn't want to do. And I looked at myself, because I had been doing it for so long, and I thought, 'I don't really know who I am. I'm so used to trying to be somebody else that I don't even know what I like; I don't know who I am.' And so I stopped, and then I got a really bad case of laryngitis, and I realized, 'I have got nobody out here.' No family, barely any friends. Nobody wanted to take me to the doctor. I called my parents, crying, and I said, 'I just want to come home.' So I went home, regrouped myself, and enrolled in online college. I did that for a little while, and then life came at me fast. I got married, had my first child at twenty-two, and have been pushing ever since. So for a while there I was lost, and didn't know what the heck I wanted to do with my life.

*

No matter how successful you become, it still sucks leaving your children at home. That never gets easy. Travel never gets easy. But I think just chipping away and inching towards whatever that passion or vision it is that you have, no matter how long it takes to stick with it, is important. One thing my mom told me when I got married was, 'Don't lose yourself inside of your marriage; always keep your passion.' She's a hairstylist and she's been one for forty-plus years now; it's her happy place. And she's always kept that with her, even raising five kids. That's something that's stuck with me. And I was always well aware I was in a position to not have to work, which was great, but I would have still lost myself. So I took some time to say to myself, 'What do I want? What am I passionate about?' And it's so funny, because what you're meant to do has usually been staring you in your face your whole life. And for me that was food. So after having my first daughter I was a bit miserable – probably leaning towards post-partum and didn't realize it – but I realized I was making my husband miserable, not giving my child good energy, and why was that? I realized it was

because, at the time, I wasn't pursuing my passion. I decided to jump into food, because that's what I've loved my whole life. I just didn't know that I could make a career out of it.

Luckily at the time, blogging was becoming a really big thing. So I said, 'Okay, I'll start a blog.' I sent the link out to just my family members, trying to keep it together and not put everything out into the world because of the insecurity that comes with putting yourself on the line. So I sent it to family, and somehow other people started to take notice, and it became a thing; people were enjoying the recipes, and from there I went to doing video and being on YouTube. I started small, like that.

Sometimes I am quick to jump in and defend myself, particularly when it comes to my kids. I will say that what you put out into the internet universe always stays there, so you have to be careful with that. Think twice, and stand behind your words. Whether you're going to get negative backlash for what you say, or positive, whatever it is, be prepared to stand behind your words, and never backtrack. That's a big thing for me.

*

I didn't necessarily have the skill sets I needed to be doing what I'm doing. So now I love to go out on a limb to help people, and grab hold of people who have that passion but may not have had the formal training or skill set they need. Because you can't learn passion, and you can't learn grit. You can learn a skill set. I really believe in that.

The way you delegate is very important as a leader, and you need to be inclusive and open, and not create consensus bias in your workspace. Making sure that your energy is very open, so that people are willing to speak up when they think that a strategy is not going to work. I think that's really important; it's something I'm looking forward to implementing in my own business. I know sometimes I get really passionate about an idea, and I tend to advocate. And I'm learning now that it's not necessarily good to be an advocator. So I'm excited to refocus and not advocate so much that people can't give me their opinions.

*

Stephen and I are those parents that aren't afraid to hug and kiss each other in front of our kids. I don't know if that's going to end up being a great thing or a bad thing. We try and keep the love in the room at all times, and not hide that from our children. We want them to appreciate love and to value that. For us, you get wrapped up in the kids and in work, so we try really hard to actually schedule our date nights and stick to them, no matter how much we're being nudged in another direction, or how much work there is to be done, or what laundry is piling up. We go. And sometimes the kids are like, 'We don't want you to leave'; we still go. We have to; it's better for them, it's great for us, and so we try and take that time. We're big on staycations, even if it's us hiring a sitter for the night and locking ourselves in our bedroom, even though most of the time we end up watching Netflix.

Parenting is hard. We were in the car the other day and [my seven-year-old] was talking about what she wants to be when she grows up. I read *Becoming*, and Michelle Obama said not to ask children what they want to be when they grow up. Because what does that mean, right? Then they have this ideal of something they have to achieve, and they don't achieve it, and then it creates anxiety and an ongoing thing of, 'I have to achieve this, and if I don't then what?' I said, 'What are you interested in?' It's always on my mind, 'Don't ask her what she wants to be.' She said, 'I want to be a singer!' I said, 'That's great! There are so many ways you can do that, so even if it doesn't happen professionally, there's always a way that you can fulfil that passion of yours.' Then I said, 'Well, what about college? What university do you want to go to?' And she said, 'I don't want to go to university.' I said, 'Do you know what university is?' She said, 'No', and I explained it to her, and she said, 'Well, I still don't want to go; I don't know why I need to go.' And I said, 'Well, you're interested in science, right? Do you know if you go to a university or college you can explore that? You could go into science if you wanted to.' And her face lit up.

These little girls don't know that there is an endless world of possibilities of different things that you can do, not *be*, but *do*, as you grow. I feel like it's my job to nurture all of her

'I'm always going to stand up for my beliefs and stand behind them.'

interests, so that she doesn't feel stuck in one thing. My parents did a great job of raising me, but I feel like at a point in time I was stuck in one thing, the acting thing, and I never had different avenues to explore. I didn't grow up with my parents having money for me to go and do activities, but still I could have explored so many different interests. I want to make sure that I nurture that for my daughter, so that *she* can decide what she wants to do.

*

In business, my milestones are important to me, the things that I achieve. But for me that isn't really success. . . . Success for me is raising these three little kids, and making sure that when they lay their heads down at night, they're happy. That's success to me. Getting through each day, and nobody has a broken bone, you know what I mean? That's success. Those are the things that keep me up at night. Is everyone safe? I'm constantly thinking about the family: Is everybody where they need to be, is everybody okay? Is all of the stuff that I'm doing affecting them in a positive way? If I can keep the answer at a yes, then that's success to me. I don't believe that there's such a thing as balance, but if there was then it would be that – being able to juggle the two things and keep everybody happy at the same time.

For the past four years my work has been for myself. I've kind of forgotten about the 'me' time. I get asked that a lot: 'When you're not with the kids, what are you doing?' 'I'm working!' I've been trying to figure out ways – even if it's ten minutes a day and I'm doing a devotional or closing my eyes and breathing – that stuff is important to me. Without that, I don't know what the heck I'd be doing.

From the podcast Girlboss Radio with Sophia Amoruso, *"Why You Can't Teach Passion or Grit, with Ayesha Curry – Chef, Author, and TV Personality," 26 June 2019*

'For me, cooking is the only way
I know how to show my love.
That's why I am so passionate
about food. It's such a love
language. Anytime I prepare a
meal for my family, I am putting
all of my time, effort, energy
and love into it. The satisfaction
you get when you see them
eating and enjoying the meal and
saying it's delicious, and you see
the smiles on everyone's faces,
I don't think anything beats that.'

The Interview

Could you please introduce yourself?

I'm Ayesha Curry. I am a mom, a wife, a believer, restaurateur, and overall entrepreneur – I like to dabble in many things.

What really matters to you?

What matters to me, truly, at the end of the day is the happiness of my children and my family. I feel like my happiness is also important, but that comes through those other two things. So, when I see that my children are happy and thriving and that my family is happy, that makes me happy, and that's what matters to me at the end of the day.

Your deepest sense of happiness comes from family?

Absolutely, yeah.

You've also talked a lot about your faith.

Oh, my faith is everything to me. I feel like it's the foundation that was set inside of me so

'If my experiences can help other people on their path to living their best life, I'm thrilled to be a part of that journey. I feel very grateful to have the platform to be able to have that kind of impact.'

young, but then at some point you go off into the world by yourself, and you're left to develop and find that faith on your own. That happened for me at a very young age and it's carried me through to where I am now, and I rely on it heavily, in the bright times and the dark times. It's that constant that's always there.

As well as being a mother and a wife, you've had a really multi-faceted career, and you've now launched a foundation. What's at the heart of your work in that space?

We launched our Eat. Learn. Play. Foundation. Children are at the helm of that, and what we want to do is ensure that every child has access to nutritious healthy food, that they have access to amazing education, and ultimately, safe spaces to play and thrive and just be kids. I feel like that's something that's being forgotten about in this day and age with how fast-paced everything is moving, and everybody has a million things to do. We're forgetting about the fundamentals of raising a child and building happy, healthy humans. So I feel like we want to make sure that those are our core pillars, and that we set that foundation so that children have the opportunity to be their best selves and live their best lives.

Did you have a particular ambition or aspiration as a young person? What were your dreams as a child?

Oh man! So, as a kid I wavered. I started out wanting to be a pulmonologist, which is a lung surgeon. My uncle's a pulmonologist and I had these hopes and dreams of curing lung cancer. I still have hope for that, to find a cure for that, but I figured out very quickly that it wasn't the space for me. I took an anatomy class in my sophomore year of high school and was bored out of my mind, and I realized I probably shouldn't be a bored doctor; that's not a smart idea. As a child I was always acting, and so I wanted to do that at a certain point, and then I realized, holy smokes, I've spent the majority of my childhood learning how to be somebody else so much so that at a certain point I forgot how to be myself and that I actually enjoyed being myself. And so

I realized that that was also not for me. Then it's one of those things where your whole life, exactly what you need to be doing is staring you in your face. That was food for me because it's such a vessel for bringing people together, and for change and communication and conversation. Ultimately it was the way that I've always made people happy.

What was at the heart of the giving and sharing of food? Were there individuals or circumstances that particularly inspired you?

I would say my mom and my grandma, but I also have this story I tell about my babysitter growing up. She was from Trinidad and she made the most amazing roti. My mom owned a hair salon in the basement of our home and her clients would get backed up because people would show up late. There'd be long waits, but people would still wait because our babysitter on Saturdays would make these rotis and bring them down. People would be so happy; you'd see them relax and sit back and be okay with the wait, and I just thought how much of a tool it was – but not necessarily in a manipulative way – in a positive way to bring them comfort and happiness and joy, and almost a sense of peace. I think that's a moment that I can pinpoint that I realized how awesome it can be.

Did you know as a child that food was going to be your 'thing'?

I didn't know it was going to be my 'thing'. I always knew it was going to be a part of me; I just didn't know that I could take that, have a career from it, and truly embrace the 'thing'. If you love what you do, you don't work a day in your life. I never believed that until I've been in it now myself, and I literally love what I do so much.

'There is no formula to finding a balance between career and motherhood. The "mom guilt" is real, but you just do your best to be present and make sure your kids always feel supported. When I'm on the road and missing home, I find some resolve in the fact that I'm setting a strong example for my daughters, showing them that with enough hard work and perseverance they are capable of anything.'

Do you have guiding principles or a driving philosophy that underpins your life and decisions?

I would say lately, yes. I didn't for a long time. I kind of just was a 'yes' woman because I wanted to make people happy, and so I'd kind of spread myself very thin. Now my principle for life is: protect your peace. That's our biggest, or my biggest, thing in life right now. It's like whatever's going to protect that for me, that's how I base my decisions. Then I also am really adamant about just doing things that make me happy, something as simple as that, but oftentimes we don't do things that make us happy. Sometimes we're going to have to do things and make decisions that we don't feel are the right way, but you know that in the end it's the right decision, and it's going to make you happy in the end. So, there's that aspect too.

When you say, 'protect your peace', are you talking about achieving a state of grace?

It's like this body, this mind that we have – we only have one of them and a lot of times with work and with just day-to-day, our mind can often get clouded, and then you feel pulled in so many different directions. So just finding out or figuring out ways to make sure you protect the space that you're in and the skin that you're in and your mental state is so important when it comes to anything, whether it's decision-making or that day-to-day process. So for me, it's just the important thing right now, and so through decision-making and what I believe in, as long as it brings me peace and it brings me joy, then I feel good in that decision, in that space.

Do you have any daily disciplines and routines you practice?

I would say prayer. I wake up, I pray, always having gratitude and giving thanks for everything, because it can be a fleeting moment and be gone in an instant. So that's really important for me to just take a deep breath in the morning, reflect on everything that's good, say a prayer, and then dive in to motherhood. That's kind of how it is for me, so I would say that's the one constant. The other maybe not-so-great ritual that I have is drinking coffee in the morning, but I think a lot of us do that!

What qualities do you think have been most critical to achieving goals during your life and career?

I would say resilience. It's not necessarily always about succeeding all of the time; it's how you recover from the failures, and I've made a lot of mistakes along the way in life and in business. For me, the tell-tale of how I'm actually doing is how I bounce back from all of the negative, so that's like the one quality I think is most important to me.

Where do you find that resilience and that
ability to bounce back?

I feel like when you're passionate about
something, and you have drive, and you have
a purpose and a mission, when roadblocks are
put in place and you hit one, for me I always
hope that that passion kicks in, and that's
what keeps me going – it kind of fills up my
tank. But my mom says it all the time – it's so
funny, she wanted to get a tattoo – 'It's okay' –
and I've told her 'no' a million times, but now
I'm thinking maybe she should get it because
whenever I do hit a roadblock that's what
I think – I'm like, 'It's okay'. You can bounce
back from that and keep it moving because
you have purpose and you have a mission
and a goal. And so whether that's not letting
anybody tell you no, or failing and realizing
you've got to keep going because of the goal,
it's okay, you can bounce back from whatever
it is that's blocking you.

'My philosophy is all about seeking joy and creating balance in life.'

What are the biggest lessons you've learned
during the course of your life and career?

The biggest lesson I think is something as
simple as, 'Nobody's perfect'. In the world
we live in right now, where perfection is what
everybody has the appetite for, nobody is
actually perfect, and for the most part that's
a façade. We live in a world today where
everybody's appetite is craving perfection,
especially with social media and all of that
stuff, and I think that the most beautiful
people in life wear their heart and their
realness on their sleeves. I think the biggest
lesson that I've learned is that it's okay to be
that person who has all of the emotions and
the insecurities and the failures, and is willing
to put that out there – because it's real.

Another lesson I've learned is that I think
in the society that we live in these days, so
many people have access to so much. One
thing my husband always says to me is – I'll
start complaining about something or I'll show
some sort of insecurity, I'll say, 'Well, they . . .', –
and he'll look and me and say, 'Well, who is
"they"?' And it's such a true statement. Who

is 'they'? At the end of the day it doesn't matter. You have the people who lift you up and hold you accountable and are there to support you physically in your life. 'They', in the grand scheme of the world, matter, but 'they', when it comes to your emotional well-being, do not. I think that's a big lesson that I've learned and am still learning.

What has been your approach when you've had to deal with failure or roadblocks?

I don't think I'm one to sugar-coat things really, ever. Sometimes it results in crying for a little while, throwing a tantrum, having a nice glass of wine. I mean that's the reality of the situation – when you fail it's not pretty: there aren't butterflies and rainbows and magical elves dancing around. It sucks when you fail. But you have your moment and then you stand up and you dust yourself off and you keep on moving. That's the easiest way I have to put it. I think we all go through the same emotions when you hit a roadblock or you fail, but again it's that resilience: you can have your moment, but then, how do you bounce back?

What does leadership mean to you?

Can I be honest? In this day and age, right
now, especially where we live currently,
I would have to say I don't believe in traditional
leadership anymore. I truly believe that the
best leaders are the greatest collaborators.
So, I am a firm believer in collaborative
leadership. I don't like hierarchies; I believe the
best things that happen are done together as
a unit. One is great, but many put together,
that's amazing. And you get more done, you
have better decision making. That's what
I believe.

That applies to your role as a mother?

It does. I think it applies to everything. In our
home, I don't make a decision by myself. It's
Stephen and me; sometimes it's the two of us
and our parents. We're very open to hearing
people's thoughts and filtering through what
we want to filter through to make the best
possible decisions as parents. And then that
goes straight into business as well. It's no
fun being by yourself, anyway, so why not

do it together? I feel like the decision making process is just better. You make smarter decisions that way.

What do you think the world needs more of?

I think the world needs more of a lot of things, but I think the world need more open hearts, just openness to possibilities. I find this day and age people are so quick to judge, and so I think the world needs more, or the people in the world need more, of an opportunity to pause and breathe and think; assess and think for themselves. I feel narratives are so skewed these days and things are right there for us to see and read and believe, but I hope that we as a society and a community can take more time to filter through things and figure them out for ourselves, so that we can form our own opinions and think for ourselves openly.

What advice would you give to twenty-year-old Ayesha?

Oh man! It's so crazy because usually it's like, 'What would you say to your twelve-year-old self?', but twenties?! I would tell my twenty-year-old self to brace for what the future holds, because with Stephen and I, we had no idea that our lives would be the way that our lives are, and I think if we could do it all over again we wouldn't change a thing. But maybe we would take a couple more deep breaths. Yeah, 'brace'.

'Beauty to me is in the eye of the beholder. Beauty comes in all different shapes, sizes, looks, qualities, but I truly believe that everybody is beautiful in their own way.'

About Ayesha Curry

Ayesha Curry is a renowned restaurateur, chef, television host and producer, and a *New York Times* best-selling author. She was born in Ontario, Canada, and moved to the United States as a teenager.

Known for her accessible approach to cooking and passion for creating easy-to-use products, her first cookbook, *The Seasoned Life: Food, Family, Faith, and the Joy of Eating Well*, was published in 2016 and became a *New York Times* bestseller, followed by *The Full Plate: Flavor-Filled, Easy Recipes for Families with No Time and a Lot to Do* in 2020. In 2017, Curry introduced her own homewares brand, AC Home Collection, which includes cookware, bakeware, kitchen textiles and a signature bedding collection, and in 2020, she launched her own lifestyle magazine, *Sweet July*.

Curry's television career includes hosting her own series, *Ayesha's Home Kitchen*, on the Food Network. She has appeared as a judge on popular Food Network shows such as *Chopped Junior* and *Guy's Grocery Games,* and served as executive producer and host of ABC's *Family Food Fight*. In 2019, she partnered with Ellen DeGeneres on *Fempire*, an EllenTube digital series that mentors young, female entrepreneurs.

As a restaurateur, Curry teamed up with award-winning chef Michael Mina to create International Smoke, a restaurant concept featuring elevated barbecue dishes from around the globe. Now with three locations across the United States, the restaurant received a Michelin Plate recognition by Michelin Guide in the first ever California edition.

In 2019, Curry and her husband, Stephen, launched their family-founded charity Eat. Learn. Play. with a mission to end childhood hunger, ensure universal access to quality education and enable healthy active lifestyles. Eat. Learn. Play. creates a new model for communities and families to come together with a commitment to unleash the potential of every child and pave the way for amazing kids and bright futures. Curry is also an ambassador for No Kid Hungry, an organization working to end childhood hunger, and is a contributing partner to Team FNV, an initiative spearheaded by Michelle Obama that aims to promote a healthy lifestyle by incorporating more fruits and vegetables into the diet.

Curry is a frequent guest on the *Rachael Ray Show* and *Good Morning America*, was a columnist for *Woman's Day Magazine,* and has been featured as a go-to lifestyle expert in publications including *Food and Wine*, *ELLE*, *Vogue*, *Forbes*, *Time*, *InStyle*, *People*, *Vanity Fair*, *USA Today*, *POPSUGAR* and more.

Curry resides in the San Francisco Bay Area with her three children, Riley, Ryan and Canon, and her husband, Stephen.

@ayeshacurry
@internationalsmoke
shophomemade.com
eatlearnplay.org

About the Project

'A true leader must work hard
to ease tensions, especially
when dealing with sensitive and
complicated issues. Extremists
normally thrive when there is
tension, and pure emotion tends
to supersede rational thinking.'

– Nelson Mandela

Inspired by Nelson Mandela, *I Know This to Be True* was
conceived to record and share what really matters for the
most inspiring leaders of our time.

I Know This to Be True is a Nelson Mandela Foundation
project anchored by original interviews with twelve
different and extraordinary leaders each year, for five
years – six men and six women – who are helping and
inspiring others through their ideas, values and work.

Royalties from sales of this book will support language
translation and free access to films, books and educational
programmes using material from the series, in all countries
with developing economies, or economies in transition,
as defined by United Nations annual classifications.

iknowthistobetrue.org

'A good head and a good heart are always a formidable combination.'

– Nelson Mandela

A special thanks to Ayesha Curry, and all the generous and inspiring individuals we call leaders who have magnanimously given their time to be part of this project.

For the Nelson Mandela Foundation:
Sello Hatang, Verne Harris, Noreen Wahome, Razia Saleh and Sahm Venter

For Blackwell & Ruth:
Geoff Blackwell, Ruth Hobday, Cameron Gibb, Nikki Addison, Olivia van Velthooven, Elizabeth Blackwell, Kate Raven, Annie Cai and Tony Coombe

We hope that together we can help to mobilize Madiba's extraordinary legacy, to the benefit of communities around the world.

A note from the photographer
The photographic portraits in this book are the result of a team effort, led by Blackwell & Ruth's talented design director Cameron Gibb. I would also like to acknowledge the on-the-ground support of Matty Wong for helping me capture these images of Ayesha Curry.

– Geoff Blackwell

About Nelson Mandela

Nelson Mandela was born in the Transkei, South Africa, on 18 July 1918. He joined the African National Congress in the early 1940s and was engaged in struggles against the ruling National Party's apartheid system for many years before being arrested in August 1962. Mandela was incarcerated for more than twenty-seven years, during which his reputation as a potent symbol of resistance for the anti-apartheid movement grew steadily. Released from prison in 1990, Mandela was jointly awarded the Nobel Peace Prize in 1993, and became South Africa's first democratically elected president in 1994. He died on 5 December 2013, at the age of ninety-five.

NELSON MANDELA
FOUNDATION
Living the legacy

About the Nelson Mandela Foundation

The Nelson Mandela Foundation is a non-profit organization founded by Nelson Mandela in 1999 as his post-presidential office. In 2007 he gave it a mandate to promote social justice through dialogue and memory work.

Its mission is to contribute to the making of a just society by mobilizing the legacy of Nelson Mandela, providing public access to information on his life and times and convening dialogue on critical social issues.

The Foundation strives to weave leadership development into all aspects of its work.

nelsonmandela.org

Sources and Permissions

1   Paige Porter Fischer, "How Ayesha Curry Scores Big with Flavor",
     Better Homes & Gardens, bhg.com/recipes/trends/how-ayesha-curry-
     scores-big-with-flavor.
2   Jonathan Borge, "Ayesha Curry rose from food blogger to culinary
     wunderkind – in just five years", *The Oprah Magazine*, 26 February
     2019, oprahmag.com/life/food/a26536429/ayesha-curry-shop-
     homemade-interview.
3   Ibid.

The publisher is grateful for literary permissions to reproduce items
subject to copyright which have been used with permission. Every effort
has been made to trace the copyright holders and the publisher apologizes
for any unintentional omission. We would be pleased to hear from any
not acknowledged here and undertake to make all reasonable efforts to
include the appropriate acknowledgement in any subsequent edition.

Pages 6, 59: Rachel Nussbaum and Jessica Radloff, "Exclusive: Chef Ayesha
Curry is the newest CoverGirl", *Glamour* magazine, 20 September 2019,
glamour.com/story/ayesha-curry-covergirl; page 12: Paige Porter Fischer, "How
Ayesha Curry Scores Big with Flavor", *Better Homes & Gardens*, bhg.com/
recipes/trends/how-ayesha-curry-scores-big-with-flavor; pages 13–14: Jonathan
Borge, "Ayesha Curry rose from food blogger to culinary wunderkind – in just
five years", *The Oprah Magazine*, 26 February 2019, oprahmag.com/life/food/
a26536429/ayesha-curry-shop-homemade-interview; page 17: Ayesha Curry, "As
a woman of color", *Instagram*, 23 January 2020, instagram.com/p/B7otFcQHoaT;
pages 19–27, 30–31: Sophia Amoruso, "Why you can't teach passion or grit,
with Ayesha Curry – chef, author, and TV personality", Girlboss Radio, 26 June
2019, girlboss.com/work/ayesha-curry-podcast-interview; page 28: Candace
Smith and Alexa Valiente, 'Why chef and entrepreneur Ayesha Curry won't
ever call herself an NBA wife', 3 January 2018, *ABC News*, abcnews.go.com/
Entertainment/chef-entrepreneur-ayesha-curry-call-nba-wife/story?id=52118573;
page 35: Lauren Sher, "Ayesha Curry shares Valentine's Day menu to make at
home", *ABC News*, 8 February 2018, abcnews.go.com/GMA/Food/ayesha-
curry-shares-valentines-day-menu-make-home/story?id=52807048; pages 39,
45: "Ayesha Curry", *Cuyana Women's Series*, cuyana.com/stories/essential-
women-ayesha-curry.html; page 50: Kristina Rodulfo, "Ayesha Curry Is the
New CoverGirl!", *PopSugar*, 20 September 2017, popsugar.com/beauty/Ayesha-
Curry-New-CoverGirl-44046045; pages 67–68: *Nelson Mandela by Himself:
The Authorised Book of Quotations* edited by Sello Hatang and Sahm Venter
(Johannesburg, South Africa: Pan Macmillan, 2017), copyright © 2011 Nelson
R. Mandela and the Nelson Mandela Foundation, used by permission of the
Nelson Mandela Foundation, Johannesburg, South Africa.

First published in the United States of America in 2021 by Chronicle Books LLC.

Produced and originated by
Blackwell and Ruth Limited
Suite 405, Ironbank,150 Karangahape Road
Auckland 1010, New Zealand
www.blackwellandruth.com

Publisher: Geoff Blackwell
Editor in Chief & Project Editor: Ruth Hobday
Design Director: Cameron Gibb
Designer & Production Coordinator: Olivia van Velthooven
Publishing Manager: Nikki Addison
Digital Publishing Manager: Elizabeth Blackwell

Library of Congress Cataloging-in-Publication Data available.

ISBN 978-1-7972-0023-1

Chronicle Books LLC
680 Second Street
San Francisco, CA 94107
www.chroniclebooks.com

10 9 8 7 6 5 4 3 2 1

Manufactured in China by 1010 Printing Ltd.

Also available in the series: